As Dr.

"When your kids leave the nest, it's your time to soar!"

Your children are gone. Now what?

In this powerful Itty Bitty Book, Dr. Dorine Kramer shares 15 Essential Tips and Tools she discovered when she was in your shoes. Discover how to be the person you want to be and live the life you want to live now that the kids are gone.

Challenges you may be facing:

- Have you lost your identity and don't know who you are anymore?
- Has your full time, 24/7 parenting role vanished, seemingly overnight, and you don't know what to do with yourself?
- Do you feel isolated, sad, perhaps embarrassed, but don't want to burden your friends and family by telling them?
- Have you become aware of distance between you and your spouse, or anxious that you're losing your connection with your adult children?

Pick up this insightful book today to redefine your identity, reinvent your role in life, restore your relationships, and redesign your future.

Your Amazing
Itty Bitty®
Empty-Nester Survival
Handbook

*15 Critical Tips To Thrive When Your Kids
Leave Home*

Dr. Dorine Kramer

Published by Itty Bitty® Publishing
A subsidiary of S & P Productions, Inc.

Printed in the United States of America

Itty Bitty® Publishing
311 Main Street, Suite D
El Segundo, CA 90245
(310) 640-8885

ISBN: 978-1-931191-70-8

I dedicate this book to my wonderful adult children, Stephanie and Benjamin, whom I love more than they can possibly know until they have children of their own. Without them I would not have had the experiences that inspired this book.

I also dedicate this book to Suzy Prudden, who was the first person I reached out to, and who believed in me until I could believe in myself; and to all you Empty-Nesters who are struggling with the changes that are inevitable during the major life transition that comes when your children leave home.

Last, but definitely not least, I dedicate this book to my husband, Nick, who has been endlessly supportive, positive, creative, and helpful, and who has encouraged me from the beginning, to go on learning, growing, and sharing what I know with the people who need me. I love you.

Feel free to drop by our Itty Bitty® website to learn more about Empty-Nesters at:

www.ittybittypublishing.com

or visit Dr. Dorine Kramer at:

www.yourtimetosoar.com

Table of Contents

Introduction

Introduction

In this Itty Bitty® Book you will find 15 essentials you need to thrive when your kids leave home, and not just to survive. Whether you are already an Empty-Nester, or whether you aren't quite there yet, everything here is relevant.

Much of what you're about to read has to do with how you treat the most important person in your life—you! Some is about how you treat other important people in your life. Every single tip is tested and non-negotiable. And every single one will make a huge difference for you if you use it.

I've done this and you can too. These essentials are the path to living the life you want, the life you deserve. Your glorious bonus is that not only will you discover your own awesomeness, but your adult children will also get to know you as the awesome person you are.

Truly, this is your time to soar. Go for it!

Step 1
This is Your Time to Soar!

If you are like most Empty-Nesters, you've spent at least the last 18 years dedicated to taking care of someone else, as your first priority. Now it's time to put yourself first. You've earned it.

1. Know that you've done a great job doing exactly what you intended—growing your child into an independent adult.
2. Your fledgling has fledged. You not only _can_ stop having her as your primary focus, you _must_ stop having her as your primary focus.
3. Raising a child is a critically important job, but the wheel of time has retired you from that one. It's time to find a new job.
4. Allow yourself to be willing to change your priorities.

1

Finding a New Role

- Like so many women, you've fulfilled your family's expectations and society's expectations. But what about your expectations? Did you want more than being a wife and a mother, however wonderful that experience has been?
- Truly, this is your opportunity. Get excited about all the possibilities you have now.
- Start looking inside yourself and outside your home for your next big adventure.
- Society often doesn't recognize you for your important contribution as a mother, so recognize yourself.
    - Give yourself a pat on the back.
    - Give yourself a hug.
    - Acknowledge yourself in words for a job well done.

Step 2
You Have Expectations, Right?

It may be counter-intuitive, but in general, the fewer expectations you have, the less likely you are to be disappointed. As an Empty-Nester, though, you must expect your child to change.

1. When your child moves out, remember this is probably the first time he has ever really needed to fend for himself in major ways. He makes his own rules for bedtimes, what he eats, even where he sleeps.
2. He is being exposed to new people, new ideas, new cultures. You don't know what they are, even if you think you do. They are bound to influence him.
3. The most important lessons he will learn with his new independence are about functioning successfully in the wider world, and finding his own way of being. This is his time to explore...and it is also yours!

Change is Inevitable

- He will always have the background and upbringing you gave him. You've provided the foundation that everything else will be based on. Now he needs to learn to function in the world outside your home, and your rules no longer apply. He will make his own.
- I know I just said to expect your child to change. What I didn't say is that even with the best will in the world, and me forewarning you, the changes can be an enormous challenge.
- The best way to approach Johnny 2.0 is twofold. First and most critical, have as few expectations as possible about anything - his friends, the clubs he joins, the classes he takes, his career choice, or anything else. And second, do your best to accept his choices without judgment, however unexpected they may be.
- You don't have to agree with his choices, but it's critical you respect them. If you don't, the door to any discussion with you or input from you will slam shut, and you run the risk of long-term damage to your relationship.

Step 3
Stay Connected—Don't Isolate

When you lose your long-standing role in life, as you do when you become an Empty-Nester, you can feel all alone. Some people handle that by actually physically isolating themselves. Some latch onto others for dear life.

1. Studies have shown that women thrive on social interaction with other women, and need to be connected to other women for emotional fulfillment.
2. Just because your kids don't go to school together anymore, that doesn't mean you can't still meet with your "school" friends. Find the ones who are going through some version of what you are, and can relate.
3. You are not alone in this experience. In addition to other parents in the same boat as you, there are people who care about you and want to be there for you. Let them!

Are You Fooling Yourself?

- You really aren't fooling anyone, except maybe yourself, if you are miserable and lonely and think you are hiding it. The people who love you all know you're sad, even if you think you're hiding it well. So let them in and let them help by being there for you.
- Isolation may make you feel safer initially, but it's all too easy for your comfy, familiar nest to become a voluntary prison. It gets harder and harder to overcome the inertia of sitting at home in front of the TV with a big bag of popcorn or a quart of ice cream.
- Remember that the characters in your favorite TV shows aren't really your friends. If you start to feel like they are, that's a warning sign that you need to make the effort to interact with real live people who can interact with you.
- Going the other direction and immersing yourself in other people's lives to avoid your pain isn't a good solution either. You must find a way to find yourself. There are some tips for that coming up...

Step 4
The Great Outdoors

If you want to feel better, get outside every day. You've probably heard about the benefits of sunshine and fresh air since you were a kid. But even if you can't always get the sunshine, getting out of your nest will help.

1. When you're feeling down, it's all too easy to plunk yourself onto the sofa and just stay there. You feel safe in your nest. It's familiar, even if it's empty and unsatisfying. The problem is that your safe space can become a trap—and you might not even notice.
2. The same scenery hour after hour, day after day, dulls your mind. That might seem like a good way to dull your pain. But is it really?
3. Studies have shown that being outdoors, particularly in green spaces like a garden, park, or forest (ooh, lucky you if you're near one of those!) can decrease stress, depression, and pain, increase creativity and memory, and encourage healing. Doesn't that sound like a better option than moping around indoors?

Get Connected to Nature

- You've no doubt heard the expression "Use it or lose it." That applies to your mind too. It's tough to get it back. I know from personal experience.
- Look at the sky, the clouds, the trees. Listen to the birds, the wind, maybe bees buzzing. Pay attention to the details. Take a few moments just to marvel at the incredible variety of life surrounding you.
- Take off your shoes and walk barefoot on grass or sand or even dirt. Your energy will change and you will feel lighter as you connect directly to the energy of the earth.
- If the best you can do is get out on your balcony, do that. Even there, the air is different. The quality of the light is different. Allow yourself the gift of feeling like a small part of a much bigger creation.

Step 5
Rhythm and Blues

Music is a universal language, like smiling. Whether you create it, play it, dance to it, or just listen to it, it has the power to uplift you, calm you, and inspire you.

1. You probably could use some uplifting, calming, and inspiring about now. Think about music you know that makes you feel good. There is no one genre of music that is better than any other. Whether it's pop, rock, spiritual, classical, rap, opera, or Broadway musicals, what you like is a personal choice. Find what works for you.
2. Sometimes the best choices are songs that you don't know yet. You can search online for suggestions matching the feeling you are looking for.
3. Make playlists for different occasions. You may want a list for when you need to calm down, another for when you want to get motivated or inspired, and another that just simply makes you feel happy.

Music Can Completely Change Your Mood

- Make sure, when you choose your music, that it isn't melancholy or bittersweet. Serious or thought provoking is fine, although lively and happy is probably better.
- Be careful when you consider your own generation's music, from your youth. A song that you loved to listen to then might evoke different feelings now, although you remember it as one of your favorites.
- An added advantage of listening to music is that it can get you up and moving. Some music just makes you want to get up and dance. That's great—Do It!
- If you sing or play music yourself, rather than just listening to it, so much the better. Stay away from the melancholy stuff and sing the inspiring stuff out loud or bang it out on the piano. It will get the oxygen moving and the juices flowing, and that can only be a good thing!

Step 6
Be A Compassionate Spouse

Remember your spouse is feeling the loss too. It may seem like you're the only one who's feeling lost, but chances are that isn't true.

1. Be kind to your spouse or partner. If she or he has been deeply involved with your child, she or he is feeling the loss too, even if you don't hear it in so many words.
2. He may not show the feeling of loss in the same ways as you. Maybe he's throwing himself into work, watching more sports, wanting more or less sex, or whatever else he always does to handle unwanted emotions. If he's acting out it's probably not about you.
3. Some people, many men in particular, are not good at talking about their emotions, so you may feel like he doesn't have any. That's probably not true. Get some professional relationship help from a coach or therapist if you aren't communicating. And don't suffer too long before you do.

Don't Give Up on Your Intimate Relationship

- This can be a challenging time for intimate relationships. If you've spent the last 18 years or more mainly discussing your child's development and activities, and planning her future, you might find yourself sitting across the table from someone you no longer know well.
- If you're feeling like strangers, wouldn't now be a good time to start getting re-acquainted?
- In the early days of your relationship, you found that person fascinating and exciting, just as they found you. What can you do today to remind yourself of those feelings?
- It takes courage, honesty and patience, but be brave, and don't give up too soon. Take the initiative. Make the effort. This relationship has been around for a while, and it can support you if you support it.

Step 7
Volunteer

One of the best ways to take the focus off how you are feeling is to take action to help solve or ease someone else's problems, or problems of society, the environment, or whatever need you see. It's rewarding in so many ways.

1. Helping and contributing can take an almost infinite number of forms. You can take your aging aunt grocery shopping. You can help provide meals for homeless people. You can do volunteer work for agencies that help the environment, animals, run-away teenagers, your local hospital, or whatever inspires you.
2. When your focus is on helping someone or something outside yourself, you feel useful, proud of yourself, and just better.
3. No matter who you choose to help, find a way to suspend any judgments of how you think the people you are serving got to the situation they are in. You don't need to know. Replace judgment with compassion and watch them and you blossom.

Volunteering Has Lots of Benefits

- Volunteering gives you a purpose and a role in life that fills, at least partially, the hole created when your 24/7 parenting role ended.
- If your confidence took a nose dive when your child left, doing helping work can give you your confidence back. You feel like you have value, because you do.
- Volunteering is an opportunity to use skills you already have, perhaps in a new way, like teaching them to others. It can also be an opportunity to gain new skills—maybe something you always wanted to do, but never did. You may find a new vocation, hobby or business interest.
- It's really hard to feel bad about yourself when you are doing volunteer work. Instead, you feel grateful that you can help and make a difference.

Step 8
Make Time Your Friend

Remember when you never had enough time because you were running around doing stuff with or for your kids? Well, your schedule isn't dictated by theirs anymore.

1. Not having your daughter's fixed school timetable in place can be a huge challenge in setting your personal timetable. You get to choose what time your day starts, what time you come home if you go out, and even when your vacations are.
2. Keep following your routine as much as possible. If you got up at 7 am to make sure your daughter had breakfast and say goodbye to her before school, keep getting up at 7 am even after she leaves home.
3. It's way too easy to slide into a habit of sleeping in late, not bothering to get dressed, and only going out for necessities or to keep up appearances. It's much harder to change that back, so don't let it happen in the first place!

Your Time is Priceless

- That's right. I said priceless. And it's so important that I'll say it again another way. Time is your most valuable, and irreplaceable, asset.
- In case you've never thought of it this way before, you only get each particular moment of your life once. And then it is gone. You really truly want to make the most of it.
- What is it that you most want to accomplish in your life? It's important to know, so take some of your valuable time to figure it out. Get help if you need it, from a coach or a counselor, but figure it out. And then use your priceless time to do it. There simply isn't anything more important!

Step 9
Rekindle Romance

Romance may not be on the top of your priority list right now, but this is great time to bump it up there. You've made a great start if you've studied Step 6. If you have a partner, romantic evenings (or mornings, or whenever) are not only a great distraction, but good for your overall health and well-being, too!

1. For romance to blossom, your non-sexual relationship with your partner also needs strengthening. Talk to each other.
2. Change something in your routine with him. Invite him to lunch on a workday, or surprise him with a loving (or maybe suggestive!) text during the day.
3. For the next 21 days, take the "Raving Fan Challenge." Do whatever you can to turn him into your "raving fan" and watch your relationship shift. Don't just assume you know what makes him feel loved and important though. Ask what he would like from you that you aren't doing. Then follow through wherever possible. And as always, make the effort not to judge anything he says.

Who's Wearing the Pants in the Family?

- During your 21 Day Challenge, notice what's working and what you appreciate about your spouse, and tell him.
- Do your best to ignore what you would normally criticize. I'm not talking about abusive words or behavior here. Those are never acceptable under any circumstances.
- Remember this is a Challenge--it *can* be tough to stick with it. It's worth it!
- Shared home-making and child-rearing is expected now, but it can unintentionally emasculate your man. That is not a good recipe for romance.
- Let your femininity out of hiding. Whatever girly things you like, do more. Bubble baths and sexy underwear, anyone?
- Help your man own his masculinity: nights out with "the boys," having a man cave, you asking him for help with a problem or decision and acknowledging him for helping.

Step 10
Speak Gently To Yourself

Have you noticed that you talk to yourself? Inside your head or out loud, you may have heard things like "I'm so useless now," or "I might as well give up," or "That was a stupid thing to do." We all have self-talk, but it's rarely positive, like "Good job!" or "Well done!" So it isn't helpful. Here's how you can and why you should change it, to thrive as an Empty-Nester – and in life.

1. If you've never paid attention to your self-talk before, set an intention to begin to notice it now.
2. You will become more aware of it, as you practice and have the intention to be aware of it.
3. Unless you are a monk, and maybe even then, you have a commentary running in your head constantly. Notice when you're being kind and encouraging to yourself, and acknowledge yourself for it.
4. When you notice you are verbally beating yourself up, stop and consciously cancel that thought. Then give yourself a truthful compliment.

Tricks of the Mind

- Your mind has some odd quirks of which you probably aren't aware, but which can derail you if you let them.
- Your mind is totally self-centered, and takes everything it hears very personally. In effect, that means that when you judge or criticize anyone, your subconscious mind makes that criticism about you. So, when you say "She's so useless" or "He's so ugly," your mind hears "I'm so useless" or "I'm so ugly."
- Does that sound like being kind to yourself? I didn't think so. Your mind does an amazing job answering questions. It will answer whatever you ask, so be sure to ask helpful questions. Ask yourself "Why am I so stupid?" and your mind will tell you exactly why you are so stupid. Then you can beat yourself up about it. If you ask, "How could I do this better next time?" you'll get expanded possibilities. Be careful what you ask.
- Your self-talk matters, so monitor it.

Step 11
Body Bliss

It's tough to feel good physically or emotionally if your body isn't at its best. It may not have been a priority when you were preoccupied with full-time motherhood, but now is the perfect time to change that. This isn't an exercise or weight loss book, but you may want to consider these ideas:

1. Use it or lose it definitely applies to strength, coordination, stamina, and brain power. I speak from experience. It's much easier to maintain your abilities than to have to regain them later.
2. Are there things you wanted to do or places you wanted to go that you put off until the kids left home? If you don't look after your body, you may lose the ability to experience those dreams. Again, speaking from personal knowledge.
3. Don't be stoic. If your body doesn't feel right, find a practitioner you can relate to, in whatever version of medical care you are comfortable with.
4. Don't hide your personal, intimate stuff out of embarrassment. Whatever problem you have, please believe me that you are not the only one who has it. Put aside your embarrassment and get it handled.

More Body Stuff

- Don't let the size or shape of your body stop you from doing what you want. Easier said than done, I know. But any potential discomfort now is better than regrets later on about what you didn't do when you had the chance.
- Consider re-evaluating what treating your body well around food actually looks like. Sometimes it really is indulging your urge for chocolate. But often that short term gratification is not a true kindness to your body.
- Pay attention to your body's signals. If you are feeling stuck and stagnant, get up and move. If you need to go pee, go now, not in half an hour when you're desperate.
- Empty-Nest and menopause often happen around the same time. If that's the case for you, be aware that some of the disturbances you feel may have a physiological origin rather than an emotional one.

Step 12
Sweet Dreams

You probably know that getting a good night's sleep can be tough when you are stressed, sad, or just in a period of transition. But did you know that poor sleep can contribute to depression, weight gain, diabetes, and a general reluctance to participate in life? Here are some guidelines.

1. Good sleep is not the same as extra hours of sleep. Neither too much nor too little sleep are good for your health, your productivity, or your mood.
2. Current research suggests that you should get about 8 hours of sleep per night. Even if you can function on less, that doesn't mean it's good for you to do so. You may be building up a sleep deficit that will catch up to you later in the form of illness or decreased health or longevity.
3. If you wake up tired, or are sleepy during the day, something is off. Don't just tolerate it. If getting to bed earlier and reducing caffeine don't fix it, or if you snore or wake frequently during the night, get help to find out and deal with what's wrong. A good night's sleep can be life-changing.

More Helpful Tidbits on Sleep

- Avoid electronics for a couple of hours before bed. The lighting can upset your biorhythms and confuse your body's sleep cycle. Some people are more sensitive to this than others, so you will have to decide for yourself if it is a problem for you.
- Be mindful of what you watch or read before bed. News, scary or violent programs, or even fantasy novels (much to my personal dismay) can give you disturbing dreams, even if they didn't used to.
- If sleep is an issue, practice good sleep hygiene by using your bed only for sleep and sex. Don't use any electronics there, even for reading or playing games.
- It's OK to take a nap during the day if you need to. Do it early in the day, though, and for not more than 20 minutes. That's long enough for a rest, and not so long that it throws you into a really deep sleep, from which it can be hard to fully come awake.

Step 13
Change Your Priorities

Even before your children were born, you made them a top priority. You may have changed your social life because alcohol was off limits. Maybe you stopped smoking or hanging out with smokers. You tried to get more rest and took special vitamins. After they were born, you just continued adapting your life to their needs, right? Me too, so I'm not judging when I say that their wants and needs probably took priority over your own. But guess what – it's time for that to change.

1. As tiny newborns, your kids are your first priority. That is a necessity. As teens, especially when it hits you that they will soon be leaving home, they somehow become even more precious.

2. The thing is, no matter how much they love you and you love them, they need and are ready to leave you behind and test their wings.

3. The harder you hang on, the more desperate they get to shake you off and prove they can manage without you. It's the classic scenario of your teenager becoming more and more belligerent and difficult so it will be easier for him to leave you.

Your Role Has Changed

- Embrace the fact that you are now in charge of only your own life. You get to do what you want and need, without having to consider when Kate's basketball competition is or when David's team is debating.
- Did you catch that? You *get to* choose!
- Your role has changed. You are now adviser, supporter, cheerleader, and mentor, not management. It might take some getting used to, but you'll get the hang of it.
- If you try to micro-manage Kate's life, you will drive yourself crazy, and at the same time, you will drive her away.
- This one's really important. David's college will help you realize you are not in charge by making all his information private (even if you are paying the bills.) Make sure you set up an emergency communication system with David, his roommate, coach, or friends, so someone lets you know if anything critical is amiss. The college won't tell you.

Step 14
You and Your Adult Child

Your children are now leading lives that they perceive as independent. However much you miss them, you need to relate to them on their terms if you want to remain welcome in their lives. Of course they miss you, but they may not want to admit to it. Here are the keys to making it easy for them.

1. Your son will make choices that you think are mistakes. Whether you agree or disagree though, it's critical that you respect his choices. If he feels judged, you won't be consulted or even informed at all the next time.

2. Be open to the new ideas your daughter is drawn to or excited about, even when they are challenging for you. Make it easy for her to discuss them with you, without judgment.

3. Watch out for subtle hidden agendas on your part. For instance, if you suggest that your son might meet his next girlfriend at events hosted by your church, he may feel you're pushing him to date women of your religious choice for your own comfort, rather than his best interests. Does he have a point? If he does, he'll balk and think you are meddling.

27

Cut Those Apron Strings!

- Your kids know you well. Even if you've put on your happy face, she knows when you are sad, like you are now. He knows it's his fault because he's leaving, and he knows he can't change that. She feels responsible and guilty, and being a relatively young human, tries to distance herself from those feelings by distancing herself from you. The more you cling when she's around, the worse she feels and the more she wants to get away.
- Of course you want to stay close and connected to your adult child. You can. You just have to do it differently now.
- The very best way to be invited and welcomed into your adult child's life is for you to grow yourself as a person. Disentangle yourself from his life and be an individual with your own passions and interests.
- Don't give unsolicited advice. Ask if she wants your help or your ideas. If the answer is no, keep them to yourself.

Step 15
What Are You Waiting For?

People find a lot of excuses, uh reasons, to delay doing what they say they want to do. How often have you heard, or possibly said, "I'll do it when I've lost 10 pounds" or "I just need to save up a little more money before I ..."? Maybe you've been saying "I'll start that after the kids leave." Well, they've left, or are about to, so what are you waiting for now?

1. Whatever you think needs to happen first probably doesn't. It's time to stop waiting and start living the life you really want.
2. I can just hear you saying "That's easier said than done." Well, you're right. But it really is worth the effort.
3. When you look more deeply at why you aren't allowing yourself to move forward, it's usually fear that's holding you back. What's the fear for you? Is it rejection? Failure? Not being good enough?
4. Another possibility is that you aren't sure what you want to do—also known as fear you will do the wrong thing. That's OK. Just start something. If it isn't fulfilling or satisfying, move on to something else.

Tips to Help You Move Forward

- Practice gratitude. Keep a gratitude journal and every night before you go to bed, jot down at least five things you are grateful for that day. Notice I didn't say *start* a journal. I said *keep* a journal. Be consistent.
- What are some activities you enjoyed before you had children? See if those are still a fit for you now. Don't give up without trying!
- Be open to opportunities that come your way. You have an enormous skill set developed over years of parenting—logistics, time management, cooking, etc. If something interests you, go for it. You are wiser and more accomplished than you know.
- Your children have left the nest. It's your time to soar! What are you waiting for?

You've finished. Before you go...

Tweet/share that you finished this book and include a picture if you can.
Please star rate this book on Amazon.
Reviews are solid gold to writers. Please take a few minutes to give us some itty bitty feedback on this book.

ABOUT THE AUTHOR

Dr. Dorine Kramer, International Speaker, Life Coach, and Author, is living proof that you can have abundance, joy, and purpose on the other side of your Empty Nest experience. She is passionate about helping moms whose children are about to leave or have already left the nest, to reinvent themselves so they know and love who they are.

After an exciting medical career, Dr. Dorine, as her colleagues and clients affectionately know her, became a stay-at-home mom by choice. When her two children, Stephanie and Benjamin, left for college, the transition from full-time mom to mom-on-the-sidelines turned into a full-blown identity crisis. She was totally unprepared for the loss of identity she felt, and the need to find a new role and focus for her life.

Now, as a life and business coach, business owner, and leader in the community, Dr. Dorine believes that women who have been putting everyone else first deserve to know, love, and value themselves and make themselves a priority. Based on her own experience, Dr. Dorine has created a unique process to help them lead amazing lives filled with purpose, passion, joy, and health.

Dr. Dorine received her medical degree from UC Irvine and her further training in public health at

UCLA. She served as an epidemiologist at the world renowned Centers for Disease Control (CDC) during the early stages of the AIDS epidemic, and as a consultant for the World Health Organization. She now lives in Southern California with her husband Nick and dog Bosco. She especially enjoys spending time with her grown kids, traveling the world, learning new stuff, and reading fantasy novels.

You can contact her at www.yourtimetosoar.com

If you enjoyed this Itty Bitty® Book you might also enjoy...

- **Your Amazing Itty Bitty® Communicating With Your Teenager Book** – Christine Alisa

- **Your Amazing Itty Bitty® Family Leadership Book** – Jacqueline T. E. Huynh

- **Your Amazing Itty Bitty® Parenting Teens Book** – Gretchen E. Downey

Or many other Itty Bitty® books published on line and available in print.

Made in United States
North Haven, CT
07 December 2022

28156763R00026